Religions of Germany and the German-Russian Volga Colonies

D. PHILIPP KAISER

Copyright 2014
by Darrel P. Kaiser
All rights reserved

First Published June 2007
by Darrel P. Kaiser
Huntsville, Alabama

Darrel Kaiser Books
www.DarrelKaiserBooks.com
email: Dar-Bet@att.net

Second Printing 2014

No part of this publication may be reproduced, stored in a retrieval system, or transmitted, in any form or by any means, electronic, mechanical, photocopying, recording, or otherwise for commercial/profit without prior written permission from author,

Exception:

The author preapproves any use or reproduction of this publication by any religious organization or person to spread GOD's word as long as this copyright page is included in all copies.

Dedication

This book, as well as any future books I may write, is dedicated to the memory of my recently passed beloved and treasured wife,

BETTY MAY KAISER

Her caring love, constant companionship, unwavering support, and unlimited patience inspired and guided me as we walked our Lord's path together, both as Best Friends for over 45 years, and as one as Man and Wife for over 40 years.

My Betty, my one and only love, still and always.
My eternal thanks… Soon we will meet again.

A Prayer for Genealogists

Lord, help me dig into the past and sift the sands of time,
That I might find the roots that made this family tree mine.
Lord, help me trace the ancient roads on which my fathers trod,
And led them through so many lands to find our present sod.

Lord, help me find an ancient book, or dusty manuscript,
That's safely hidden now away in some forgotten crypt.
Lord, let it bridge the gap that haunts my soul when I can't find,
The missing link between some name that ends the same as mine.

Curtis Woods

Preface

The book attempts to search out the different factors that led to the development of religion in our German-Russian ancestors.

The First Chapter covers pre-history in Germania to about 1765. The Second Chapter covers the Büdingen Connection to the Volga Colonists. The Third Chapter covers the First hundred Years in the Volga Colonies. The Fourth Chapter is a pictorial of some of the beautiful churches that were built in the German-Russian Volga Colonies. Chapter Five is called "All Things Must Change" and covers the loss of Religious freedoms from around 1861 thru just before World War II. A Bibliography and Endnotes complete this book.

This book is one in a series of books on the German-Russians of the Volga Colonies. For more information on the Volga Colonies, some of my other books are:

"Origin & Ancestors Families Karle & Kaiser of the German-Russian Volga Colonies"

"The Bad & Downright Ugly of the German-Russian Volga Colonies"

"Moscow's Final Solution: The Genocide of the German-Russian Volga Colonies"

"Emigration to and from the German-Russian Volga Colonies"

For information on this and other books I have written on a variety of topics including more on the German-Russian Volga Colonies, Watercolor quilts, basic electrical troubleshooting, sewing machine maintenance, the original Sewhandy sewing machine, and the SINGER Model 221 Featherweight…. Please visit my websites at

www.DarrelKaiserBooks.com
www.Volga-Germans.com

Your comments and/or submissions to improve this book are always appreciated. Discussions as to the validity of my theories and assumptions are welcome. Submission of copies of photographs or documents that are applicable to the subject is encouraged, and credit will be given in the next edition.

Email me with any and all comments or questions at

Dar-Bet@att.net

I sincerely hope you find this book interesting and educational!

Table of Contents

Dedication

Preface

Chapter I: Religion in Germany — *1*

Chapter II: The Büdingen Connection — *46*

Chapter III: The First Hundred Years in the Volga Colonies — *48*

Chapter IV: Churches of the Volga Colonies — *69*

Chapter V: All Things Must Change — *88*

Summary — *91*

Bibliography — *92*

End Notes — *97*

Chapter I
Religion in Germany

Life in Rural Germany Today

How important was religion to my Volga German-Russian ancestors? My time in Germany leads me to believe that nothing in their lives was more important...

My wife and I lived in the small rural farming village of Hoppachshof, Kreis Schweinfurt, Bavaria, Germany for a little over two years. When we first arrived in 2003, we attended their annual Kirchweihe or parish fair or community church party. Everyone in the village comes and I do mean everyone. It was a great way to get to know the local people.

There was a huge tent with rows and rows of tables and benches. It seemed to be overflowing with both happy people, all sorts of meats, and German beer. German music and song filled your ears. Even though my wife and I were village newcomers, we were enthusiastically welcomed to join an already full table. We sat down to a variety of foods and beer and enjoyed the culture and music.

During one of those rare lapses of music, in polite conversation I was asked, "What religion are you?" It got kind of quiet around the table while they all waited for my answer. I thought to myself that it was a strange question, and decided to ignore it. Then I looked around and realized that they all wanted an answer. I replied that I was baptized and confirmed Lutheran.... Dead Silence... Long extended pause... Talk about feeling uncomfortable.

And then someone said, "Hoppachshof is a Catholic Village." He continued "that we were welcome to attend their village church anyway, because a Lutheran is ALMOST a Catholic, and that after a while they would get us to come back to the correct Catholic side". With that, everyone laughed, and the fun continued. We were considered wayward Catholics.

While Hoppachshof was Catholic, the nearest Protestant church (called Evangelical in Germany) is about five miles distant in a Protestant village. Again, this illustrates the importance of Religion in rural Germany even today.

Religion remains a day-to-day part of their lives in rural Germany. The bells ring on the hour, and ring even more often to call the villagers to the church for worship. I have never experienced anything like this in my travels across the US. These experiences were in Present day Germany in 2003 thru 2005.

My experiences were primarily in the rural part of Bavaria, Germany. They would not be the norm in urban Germany today. It is estimated that there are about 26.5 million Catholics and 26.2 million Protestants in Germany making up almost two thirds of the population. However, the Religions are losing 200,000 to 300,000 members every year. Since 1973, the Evangelical Church has lost over 4 million members.[1]

How does this apply to my German-Russian ancestors? Modern urban Germany does not. I do think that rural Germany still gives us a glimpse of the role Religion played in my German ancestor's lives. I know that 250 years ago, Religion was even a more important part of my ancestor's day-to-day lives. History tells us that Religion was definitely even more "important" about 400 years earlier during the Thirty Years War when German Catholics and Protestants were killing each other by the thousands in northern Bavaria, Hesse, and Isenburg.

Religion

Religion is universal. For as long as it could be recorded, man has always given some type of recognition to a power or powers beyond himself.[2]

Religion is also one of the few things that separate us from the animal world.[3]

Religion gives to any person something he cannot get anywhere else. That is a confidence in the final outcome of the struggles of life through a personal connection with the Superior power or powers overseeing the world. It is because of the daily challenges that religion continues to exist.

Religion is the common tool to help us explain the reasons for things that we do not or cannot understand through the context our known physical world.[4] It offers hope in the face of uncontrollable situations. It outlines an ideal society and enhances quality of life.[5]

The practice of religion is infinitely varied. It means different things to different peoples. To the primitive man, it might mean the offering of sacrifices to his gods. To an aborigine, it might be in the mutilation of his own body. For my ancient Celtic ancestors it was the Druids, for the Greeks it was their gods, for the Germanics it may have been shamanistic. And much later of course, it was the Roman Catholic

Church and Papacy, and the Protestants with all of its branching faiths.[6]

While there is a multitude of religions throughout the present-day world, and there were even more in the ancient world, I am focusing on the religions that were probably practiced by my German Ancestors as they evolved over the eons. These religions include Polytheism (Celts), Animism & Shamanism (Germanics), Polytheism (Roman), and of course, Catholic, Protestant, and the Reformed Faiths.

It has always puzzled me that something as pure and good as the concept of the belief in a higher being, GOD, could be somehow twisted into the reason for the killing of other human beings. Of course, strong faith does go hand-in-hand with strong emotions... It would seem that it is the variety of Religions that is the problem..... over the thousands of years of history we as a race have usually believed that our personal interpretation of GOD or Religion is the only "correct one."

Ardently believing that our Religion is the only "correct one," it is logical to think that we have a responsibility to help others learn that ours is the only correct one. How far we "push" our beliefs on others is one problem. Another problem is that other (misguided) people have the mistaken belief that their Religion is the only way to GOD. So there you have it with people believing differently and people forcing others to believe as they do.

Even with this logic, it was still difficult to rationalize the murder of unbelievers. Someone finally explained it clearly to me when I was in Baghdad, Iraq. He told me that he would be doing my soul a "favor" if he killed me and sent me back to GOD. This would give my "soul" another chance to be born again on Earth to hopefully believe correctly in his Religion.

Carry this idea to the extreme and you have a Religious War. This can be the military forces of one country or countries with established religion against those of another country or countries with either a quite different religion or a different sect. It can also be group or faction not associated with a specific country driven to spread its faith by violence.

Before I move into the discussion of the actual religions, I want to make sure that the purpose of this book is clear. The goal of this book is to identify how my ancestors' religions developed, the similarities and differences of the religions they practiced, and the impact of their religious faith on their customs and daily lives. It is not meant to be a discussion into which religion is right or wrong, or better or best. I am not qualified to offer an opinion on that.

Religion in Pre-History Germany
Celtic –Polytheism

Polytheism is the belief in or worship of multiple gods or divinities. Most ancient religions were polytheistic, holding to pantheons[a] of traditional gods. These were accumulated over centuries.

---

[a] The set of all the gods of a particular religion or mythology.

Note that the belief in many gods does not preclude the belief in one all-powerful all-knowing Supreme Being (Top God). Most ancient religions were polytheistic. One that was not was the henotheistic Greek and the Roman Classical Pantheon of gods. That will be covered later in this section.[7]

There really is not much left to tell us about the Celt religion. Using other groups of the same time, religious scholars have reconstructed what the Celt religion was probably like.[8] The Celts were polytheistic; these gods were ultimately derived from more primitive Indo-European sources that gave rise to the polytheistic religions of Greece, Persia, and India.[9]

Some consider the Celtic religion to be one of Animism, as the Celts believed that gods and goddesses inhabited every natural feature and phenomenon. The earliest aspect of their religion was a cult of nature spirits or of the life manifested in nature. It is thought that the religion of the Celts was a religion of Ethics, Nature and Knowledge or science, and one with a mythology that included the idea of transmigration of the soul or reincarnation.[10]

Celt men and women probably had separate cults, and probably the women's' was more important. As hunters of animals men worshipped what they slew, apologizing to the animal for the necessary slaughter. This "apology" concept is found repeatedly in many primitive hunter societies. Animals that they felt were too sacred to be slain would be preserved and worshipped.

This might have given birth to domestication and pastoral life, with totemism[b] as the most likely cause. Earth, giving us vegetation, was the fruitful mother (Mother Earth). Since the origin of agriculture is mainly due to women, the Earth cult would be practiced by women. Later vegetation and corn spirits, all regarded as female, would be added. As men branched out into agriculture, they would join in the female based cults.

With the growth of religion, the vaguer spirits tended to become gods and goddesses, and sacred animals to become anthropomorphic[c] divinities, with the animals as their symbols, attendants, or victims. Vegetation spirits centered in the ritual of planting and sowing, and so developed divinities of growth centered in great seasonal and agricultural festivals.

It was not all peaceful because migrating Celts also conquered new lands. They also evolved many divinities of war. In spite of worshipping so many local war-gods, the Celts were not merely men of war. Normally they engaged in war only when need arose, with agriculture and animal farming always the priority.[11]

We do know that Celtic gods tended to come in threes; the Celtic logic of divinity usually centered on triads. This triadic logic probably had tremendous significance in the translation of Christianity into northern European cultural models.[12] This idea of the *Third Force,* as represented by

---

[b] The belief that people are descended from animals, plants, and other natural objects.

[c] The attribution of human characteristics and qualities to non-human beings, objects or natural phenomena such as animals, forces of nature, or believing in an unseen author of things.

the Triskele,[d] can be seen on Celtic artifacts, including coins.[13] Most of the Celtic gods were local in character with each tribe possessing its own group.

Because they were of the same origin and interaction, each god might have functions similar to those of other groups. Some eventually gained a universal character over time and absorbed lesser-known gods. And over time, the primitive nature-spirits gave place to greater or lesser gods, each with his separate department and functions. Growing civilization began to separate the Celts from the soil, but they never quite lost touch with it. The Celts believed in unseen gods, and they believed in an unseen region where they passed after death.[14]

It appears to some that the Celts did not love their gods, but feared them and felt it necessary to negotiate and placate them in order to forestall their wrath. According to Julius Caesar, who gives the longest account of druids, the center of Celtic belief was the passing of souls from one body to another. From an archaeological perspective, it is clear that the Celts believed in an after-life since material goods are buried with the dead.[15]

Eventually, over a long period, the Celts learned of and accepted ancient Christianity.[16] While nothing about how this conversion to Christianity is left in Europe, there is a vast amount of information available about the Celts in Great Britain and their conversion to a Celtic Christianity. Odds are that the conversion happened quite similarly.

Celtic religious life had a more or less organized special class, called the druides or "druids" by the Romans. We do

---

[d] Symbol of the triple spiral.

not know what the Celts called them. Very little is actually known, but here is what is theorized: As a special group, the druids performed many of the functions that we would consider "priestly" functions, including ritual and sacrifice, kind of like our current ministers and priests. However, they also included functions that we would place under "education" and "law", similar to that of our teachers and judges. Their rituals and practices were probably kept secret which was tradition common among early Indo-European peoples.

The most widely accepted information about the Celts is that the druids performed "barbaric" or "horrid" rituals at lakes and groves. While that may be true at times, it does not appear to have been a prevalent practice.

If the "barbaric" or "horrid" rituals rumors were not true, how did they come about? It most likely is bad publicity provided by their enemies, the Greeks and Romans (who killed and tortured unknown thousands during their time in power).[17]

This brings to mind three comments, 1) The winners always rewrite history to favor themselves and make the losers look worse than they actually were, 2) this is kind of like the "pot calling the kettle black," and 3) motion picture industry "historical" movies may have helped spread the rumors.

Germanics

The term Germanics covers a huge group. Some of the tribes may have been Polytheistic and worshipped similar to the Celts. Others may have followed Animism or Shamanism. A Germanic example of Polytheistic might be the Inguaeones. These were West Germanics.

The name Inguaeones is derived from the god Inguz from whom they believed they had descended. Inguz is another name for the Germanic god Freyr. Among the Norse, Freyr is revered as the brother of Feya, or Frigga - wife of Odin. Other tribes belonging to the Inguaeones were the Jutes, Frisians, Warns, Angles, and the Saxons. The Inguaeones seemed to follow a line of gods similar to those of the Norse with Odin being the supreme god. All Inguaeones lived in the coastal areas along the North Sea in an area that roughly covers South Scandinavia, Denmark and the Weser/Oder region.[18]

Animism

The basis for animism is agreement that there is a spiritual realm which humans share the universe with. The ideas that we possess souls, and that our souls have life apart from our human bodies, before and after death, are central parts of animism. Additionally, animism believes that animals, plants, and celestial bodies also have spirits.[19]

Animistic gods are often immortalized with mythology explaining the creation of fire, wind, water, man, animals, and other natural earthly things. Although the beliefs of animism can vary widely, similarities between the characteristics of gods and goddesses and rituals practiced by animistic societies exist.[20]

Shamanism

Shamanism is a range of traditional beliefs and practices that involve the ability to diagnose, cure, and sometimes cause human suffering by traversing the "axis mundi"[e] and forming a special relationship or gaining control over spirits.

---

[e] Center of the world and/or the connection between heaven and earth..

Followers have been credited with the ability to control the weather, divination, the interpretation of dreams, astral projection, and traveling to upper and lower worlds.

These beliefs have existed throughout the world since prehistoric times. Shamanism is based on the idea that the visible world has invisible forces or spirits that can affect the lives of the living. This practice requires specialized knowledge or abilities, and it might be appropriate to say shamans are the experts used by animist communities. [21]

Rome – Polytheism

Greek and Roman religion took the form of a monarchical polytheism. Zeus or Jupiter was the supreme all-powerful and all knowing king and father of the all the Olympian gods. The Philosophers Plato and Plotinus respectively taught that above the gods of traditional belief was "The One". The One is the impersonal unifying principle of divinity.[22]

The origins of the Roman religion began with the small farming community of Rome. The foundations included nameless and faceless deities that lent support to the community while inhabiting all objects and living things. Numen, as the belief in a pantheistic inhabitation of all things is called, would later take root in more clearly defined system of gods, but early on, the belief that everything was inhabited by numina was the accepted path.[23]

The early Romans were not very concerned with the distinct personalities of each god, but there were rules outlining what each particular deity was responsible for. All aspects of life were guided. The Roman gods and goddesses were usually a blend of several religious influences. Many were introduced by the Greeks and others by the Etruscan or Latin tribes of the region.

The gods of the Roman religion began taking on the forms known today around 6th century BC. These gods, Jupiter (Zeus), Juno (Hera), and Minerva (Athena), were worshiped at the grand temple.

As Rome's power grew and expanded throughout the known world, they came into contact with the cultures and religious beliefs of many other cultures. The Romans society and religion absorbed and assimilated any culture they felt could be beneficial. This included even "Foreign gods". With the passing of the Roman Republic into that of an Imperial system, Roman religion expanded to include the Emperors themselves.

Julius Caesar, having claimed to be a direct descendent of Aeneas the son of Venus, was among the first to deify himself in such a manner. At first, such a system of human divinity was largely rejected by the masses, but the popularity of Caesar helped pave the way for future leaders.[24] This system existed "as is" for many centuries.

Eventually, all good and bad things come to an end. Christianity slowly arrived, and even though it was severely persecuted, grew in popularity and numbers of followers. History tells us that in 312 AD, Roman Emperor Constantine had a "miraculous conversion" to Christianity. And so the Roman Catholic Church was born.

One might wonder that the "miraculous conversion" in 312 AD might have been more political, and less miraculous. I have no doubt that by this time, Emperor Constantine realized that 1) Christianity wasn't just going to go away, 2) Continued persecution of Christians would continue to weaken his power, and 3) if you can't beat them, then join them. His conversion ensured the Rome power base so successfully that it still exists today with the Papacy.

From 312 until his death in 337, Constantine was simultaneously building pagan temples and Christian churches, but was slowly turning over the reigns of his pagan priesthood to the Bishop of Rome. With Constantine's emphasis on making his newfound Christianity acceptable to the heathen in the Empire, the "Christianization" of Roman deities was begun.

Unfortunately, not all was well in Rome. Christians were still being persecuted, only now it would be for not agreeing with the Roman Catholic version backed by the Emperor who was acting in the name of Jesus Christ.[25] Officially, Christianity was not made the official religion of the Roman Empire until the edicts of Theodosius I in 380 and 381 A.D. More on this in the Christianity section below.

Christianity

For this book, a "*Christian*" includes any group or individual who seriously, devoutly, prayerfully describes themselves as Christian. That may not be your definition, so be it. Under this definition, Christianity includes Roman Catholics, Protestants, Southern Baptists, Jehovah's Witnesses, Mormons, United Church members, etc.[26] Christianity is based upon the teachings of Jesus Christ, a Jew who lived his life in the Roman province of Palestine.[27]

Christianity has gone through many transformations since the execution of Jesus circa 30 CE. Except for its first few half decade (circa 30 to 35 CE), Christianity has never been a single, unified religion. Immediately after Jesus' death, his disciples formed a reform group within Judaism, normally referred to as Jewish Christianity. This new religion was centered in Jerusalem.[28] Roman communications networks enabled Christianity to spread quickly throughout the Roman Empire and eventually to the rest of Europe, and finally the entire globe.

By around 36 AD, primitive Christianity had three major branches,[29] 1) Jewish Christianity, 2) Gnostic Christianity, and 3) Pauline Christianity.[30] Unfortunately, the relationship between the Roman Catholic Church and other religions has historically been stormy.[31]

Jewish Christianity/Messianic Judaism

Messianic Jews/Jewish Christians hold to certain Jewish practices while believing that Jesus (whom they call by his Aramaic name "Yeshua") is the Savior that was predicted in the Hebrew Scriptures. The earliest Christians were Jewish Christians whose missions were directed towards the Jews. By the fourth century there were almost no distinctively Jewish congregations left.[32]

There are important differences between the teachings of Jesus as taught by James, and those taught by Paul. Some have explained the main difference in terms of the "audience". Jesus preached primarily to Jews. He spoke and acted against what he believed was corruption in Herod's Temple and 1st century Judaism, which Josephus divided into Sadducee, Pharisee and Essene sects.

James continued this teaching focus as leader of the Jerusalem Church with both Aramaic and Greek speakers.

Those that support this explanation believe that Paul, as the "Apostle to the Gentiles," took the teachings of Jesus and made them relevant and interesting to the polytheistic Roman gentiles.

They also feel that in order for this to succeed and gain popular support, Paul had to merge the teachings of Jesus and the Christian religion with certain characteristics common to the other gods and religions of that time.[33] Because of this, they felt that the Christianity of Paul (later known as Pauline Christianity) was wrong.

Gnostic Christianity

Followers of Gnostic Christianity feel their religion is based on the original teachings of Jesus. A Gnostic believes that salvation is gained through the acquisition of divine knowledge or gnosis, and that the knowledge necessary for salvation has already been revealed through Jesus. They also feel that our world is subject to powers of darkness that distort our concept of reality.

When Gnostics refer to salvation, they mean being freed from these illusions of darkness so that they can perceive the True Reality. They believe that when Jesus used symbolic parables to urge his hearers to search for the knowledge of Truth, he privately entrusted to his disciples the gnosis or experiential knowledge which they could share only with those who became their fellow disciples.[34]

Pauline Christianity

As I wrote above, some Christians see Pauline Christianity as compromise and merging of Messianic Jews/Jewish Christian and polytheistic Roman beliefs. Of the three types,

Pauline is the one that Rome decided to support and make tax exempt,[35] and eventually eradicated the other two.[36]

Pauline Christianity grew to become the Roman Empire's state religion late in the fourth century AD. State funds and Church funds eventually merged into one. The church then attained a near monopoly within the Empire. They persecuted the Jews, and wiped out other competing religious voices: Gnostic Christianity, the Mystery Religions, the various other Pagan religions, etc. They used any means they felt necessary, and forcibly converted, exterminated, or exiled the leaders of other faith groups.

Even centuries later, threats (real or imagined) to the Roman Catholic Church were typically solved through intimidation or violence. Good examples are the Crusades with their "offer" of convert or die.[37] To be fair, history has recorded examples of most all Religions losing control and torturing, banishing or killing those suspected of not believing as those in power did.

The Roman Catholic Church centers itself on the Pope, or spiritual leader. He traces his office's lineage back to the first Pope, St. Peter, one of Jesus' disciples.

All Popes are believed by the Church to be or have been the Interpreter and Expounder of GOD. They are felt to also be "infallible" but only if three conditions are met: 1) The Pope must speak ex cathedra, or from the Chair of Peter, in his official capacity; 2) The decision must be binding on the whole church; and 3) It must be on a matter of faith and morals. Outside of those conditions, the Pope is as likely to make mistakes as you or I.

Note that Politics was not included in the above conditions. Maybe if the Popes' had limited themselves only to their "infallible" areas, there might never have been born the religions that split away from the Roman Catholic Church.[38]

However, the Popes did not limit themselves, and during the fourth century, the Roman Catholic Church split and the Eastern Orthodox branch was formed. This split was primarily a political one due to the division of the Roman Empire into western and eastern components. The two churches became officially separate in 1054.[39]

Roman Catholic

The Roman Catholic Church believes that it is both organizationally and doctrinally the original Christian Church, founded by Jesus Christ.[40] This is also claimed and disputed by the Eastern Orthodox Church, and by the Protestants.

The Church has always been a hierarchical organization in which ordained clergy are divided into the orders of bishops, priests, and deacons. The See of Rome has always been pre-eminent in the Church (except for the period when it was in Avignon, France), because it is the seat of the bishop, known as the Pope, whom Catholics consider to be the successor of Saint Peter, the chief of the Apostles (sometimes titled the "Prince of the Apostles").[41]

A prominent figure in the Christianization of the German tribes,[42] considered the father of German Christianity, was the English missionary Saint Boniface (675-754 AD).[43] The illustration on the next page is an artist drawing from the early 1900's of a 700 AD meting in Saxony.[44]

Supposedly, Boniface found a tribe worshipping a Norse deity in the form of a huge oak tree. He marched up to the tree, took off his shirt, and grabbed an axe. Without a word, he hacked down their six-foot wide wooden god/tree. He stood on the trunk, and is quoted as asking, *"How stands your mighty god? My God is stronger than he."* The crowd's reaction was predictable, though that they did not kill him.

Saint Boniface was also known as Winfrid, Wynfrith, and the Apostle of Germany.[45] One story about him says that he used local tribal customs to help convert them to Christianity. A tribe had a game in which they threw sticks called *kegels* at smaller sticks called *heides*. Boniface adapted religion to the game, with the *heides* representing demons, and then knocking them down to show purity of spirit.[46]

Saint Boniface [47]

The historical relationship of the Pope and the Emperor of the Holy Roman Empire has been rocky at best. At times over more than a thousand years, both parties tried gain for themselves complete control of both the earthly and spiritual authority. But, it can be truthfully said that the armies of the Holy Roman Empire were the enforcement arm of the Pope. Whether the Roman Catholic Church would have survived and prospered without the military support of the Holy Roman Empire is a good question.

It is certain that without the repeated "forced" conversion of "unbelievers" to Catholicism using the "convert or die" approach, there would most likely be a lot less Catholics (and Christians). Remember the rumor that Celtic Druids performed human sacrifices. Weigh that against the known facts that thousands were tortured and put to death on orders of the Roman Catholic Church.

A good example of the bond of the Pope and the Emperor of the Holy Roman Empire was Charlemagne (768 AD – 814 AD). He ruled the Franks for forty-three years and was Emperor of the West for 14 years.[48] His goal was to solidify his power by removing any contenders, and to convert all to Christianity.[49]

However, not everyone felt the same and problems arose quickly. The other Germanic tribe leaders did not willingly give up their power and kingdoms, or the Pagan religion of their ancestors.[50] What did Charlemagne do? He forcibly annexed southern Germany, conquered Lombardy and Saxony, and converted the pagans to Christianity.

In 772 AD, Charlemagne moved to conquer the Saxons at his eastern border, and to convert them to the Christian faith. The Saxons, led by "Duke" Widukind did not agree to accept Christianity. Even though "Duke" Widukind had pledged his allegiance to Charlemagne, he had not agreed to give up the Pagan ways. Hostilities between the two allies continued. In

Charlemagne [51]

782 AD, the Saxons defeated and annihilated a large Frankish occupying army. Later after another battle (or bloodbath), this time near Verdun, Charlemagne was victorious.[52] "Duke" Widukind was forced to flee for his life to Denmark, but Charlemagne took between 4000 - 5000 Saxon warrior prisoners.[53]

Charlemagne accepting Widikund surrender [54]

The blood-bath name came about because Charlemagne is reported to have revenged an earlier massacre of young noble Franks by decapitating all 4000 to 5000 Saxon prisoners in a single day.[55] It is reported that all were killed without mercy. This terrible act finally broke the Saxon will to fight, and it earned Charlemagne the nickname "Butcher of the Saxons".[56]

Great emphasis was placed on missionary work and conversion to Christianity; however, many of his Franks kept hidden their pagan beliefs. Considering the reputation of Charlemagne, that is not surprising. History records his reign as a fanatical struggle for power and religion with the other Germanic tribes.

Charlemagne teaching Christianity [57]

In 785 AD, Charlemagne had Widukind and all his followers christened as Christians "in their absence." This is supposedly the first time where a whole people became Christians by the threat of force. Resistance flared again in

792 AD, and this time Charlemagne ended it by deporting parts of the Saxon people to other areas.[58] This is not the finest example of helping convert unbelievers to Christianity.

In 799 AD, the Roman Papacy was consumed with politics and power. Powerful rival noblemen in Rome imprisoned Pope Leo III on charges of criminality. However, the Pope escaped to the safety of the city of Paderborn that was under the control of Charlemagne.[59]

From that time on, the Pope and Charlemagne were close allies. And on Christmas Day 800 AD, Pope Leo III crowned Charlemagne in a papal coronation as the Holy Roman Emperor of all the Roman territory, including that from the Pyrenees to Bohemia and from Schleswig to Rome.[60]

The alliance between the Emperor, a temporary ruler backed by the military, and the Pope of the Roman Catholic Church, who provided the spiritual side of the imperial mission, gave this combined government almost unlimited power. That is as long as they both agreed on how to rule![61] The kingdom of Charlemagne grew to include what today is known as France, the Netherlands, Belgium and Luxembourg, most of Germany and Austria and northern parts of Spain and Italy. It would later be known as the "First Reich."[62]

The years from 1305 to 1378 were a time of much confusion in the Roman Catholic Church. The period is known as the Avignon Papacy, and was when the Bishop of Rome or Pope, lived in Avignon, France[63] instead of Rome, Italy.

Seven popes, who just happened to all be French, resided in Avignon during this time: Pope Clement V: 1305–1314, Pope John XXII: 1316–1334, Pope Benedict XII: 1334–1342, Pope Clement VI: 1342–1352, Pope Innocent VI: 1352–1362, Pope Urban V: 1362–1370, and Pope Gregory XI: 1370–1378.

In 1378, Gregory XI moved the papal residence back to Rome, Italy and died there. There were still arguments within the Church as to who was in charge where, and a faction of church cardinals actually set up an antipope back in Avignon, France.

This was the beginning of the period of Catholic Church confusion from 1378 to 1414 that Catholic scholars refer to as the "Western schism" or "the great controversy of the antipopes". This time is also called "the second great schism" by some secular and Protestant historians. The Catholic Council of Constance in 1414 finally resolved the controversy and did away with the Avignon papacy.[64]

Avignon Papal Palace [65]

Eastern Orthodox

Followers of The Eastern Orthodox Church also trace their common origins back to Christ and the Apostles through unbroken Apostolic Succession. As noted above, in the first thousand years of Christianity both churches were united. They followed identical doctrine with slight differences in style of worship.

Following a long period of political squabbling from 800 to 1000 AD, certain doctrinal and political differences arose that eventually lead to the Great Schism in 1054.

Eventually the Eastern Church adopted the name "Orthodox" to reinforce its claim to be the preserver of the original Christian traditions as well as those established by the church during the first 1000 years of its existence.

Orthodox churches are largely national, each associated with a particular country. Orthodoxy is common in Russia, Greece, Romania, Bulgaria, the Ukraine, and Armenia. The influence of the Orthodox Church encompasses the territories associated with the Byzantine Empire: Eastern Europe, Asia (Russia/Siberia), parts of the Middle East and Africa.[66]

The Reformation

The Protestant branch split off from Roman Catholicism during series of 16th and 17th century church reforms in doctrine and practice. Martin Luther started this movement, called the Reformation. It challenged the authority of the Pope. There were others connected with this Europe-wide movement such as John Wycliffe, John Huss, Ulrich Zwingli, John Calvin, and John Knox.

Martin Luther is best known as the "Father of Enlightenment" in Germany. He was born into the transition from the Middle Ages and the Modern Ages. As an Augustinian monk, he was concerned about the worldly connections and indulgences within the Catholic Church.

His complaints about the Catholic Church were an effort to bring the church back to the "pure way" and were not intended to spark a movement. His actions did start a religious movement that spread through out Europe.[67] The Church rebuked Martin Luther, but he continued to suggest methods on how to improve the church.

Everything changed over the financing of the lavish building program of Saint Peter's Basilica in Rome. The Pope was selling Indulgences to the wealthy. Indulgences were a way for one to spend less time or no time in Purgatory. At this time the people did not worry about whether they were going to hell; they felt sure they would. The question was about how long they would be in Purgatory. Those wealthy enough to be able to buy an indulgence could get out of Purgatory (or so the Church promised). Supposedly, it worked like a "Get out of Jail Free" Card used when playing a kids' table game.

Some religious leaders even sold Indulgences to the families of the deceased to limit their loved ones time in hell. These indulgences were very important for the papacy because next to the earnings from the lands the Church owned, they were its major income source. However, the poor could not afford indulgences. The obvious logic here is that wealthy people get to purchase Heaven, but the poor people will go to Hell.

At this time, the papacy needed more money for building St. Peter's Basilica and to finance wars (especially the Crusades that were needed to convert or kill all the unbelievers). When Luther learned of this, he became even more outspoken.

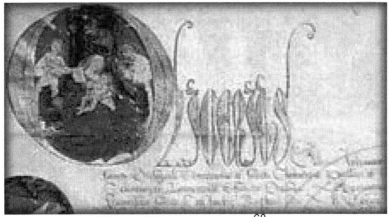
Papal Indulgence [68]

Get out of Jail Free Card [69]

A present day explanation by the Catholic Church states that the primary reason for selling of Indulgences was to allow a person to limit or eliminate any temporal or earthly punishment that the Church might levy.

The Church explains that the Indulgence was never to eliminate a living persons' future time in Purgatory or guarantee admission to Heaven. While Indulgences were sold to people so their ancestors might have less time in Purgatory, the present Church explains that GOD may or may not use the indulgence to benefit a particular ancestor as GOD sees fit.[70]

It would appear that "today's" limited definition of Indulgences was not in use in the time of Martin Luther. If they had been, he might never have broken away from Catholicism.

It would also appear that if "today's" limited definition of Indulgences was in use in the time of Martin Luther, no one, wealthy or poor, would have purchased Indulgences. So much for the current Church explanation.

In 1517, Luther posted his 95 Thesis on the Wittenberg castle church door (a legend?) protesting, for theological reasons, the sale of indulgences to finance the pope's schemes.[71]

95 Thesis of Dr. Martin Luther, 1517

"Out of love for the truth and the desire to bring it to light, the following propositions will be discussed at Wittenberg, under the presidency of the Reverend Father Martin Luther, Master of Arts and Sacred Theology, and Lecturer in Ordinary on the same at that place. Wherefore, he requests that those who are unable to be present and debate orally with us, may do so by letter."

In the Name our Lord Jesus Christ. Amen.

1. Our Lord and Master Jesus Christ, when He said Poenitentiam agite, willed that the whole life of believers should be repentance.

2. This word cannot be understood to mean sacramental penance, i.e., confession and satisfaction, which is administered by the priests.

3. Yet it means not inward repentance only; nay, there is no inward repentance which does not outwardly work divers mortifications of the flesh.

4. The penalty [of sin], therefore, continues so long as hatred of self continues; for this is the true inward repentance, and continues until our entrance into the kingdom of heaven.

5. The pope does not intend to remit, and cannot remit any penalties other than those which he has imposed either by his own authority or by that of the Canons.

6. The pope cannot remit any guilt, except by declaring that it has been remitted by God and by assenting to God's remission; though, to be sure, he may grant remission in cases reserved to his judgment. If his right to grant remission in such cases were despised, the guilt would remain entirely unforgiven.

7. God remits guilt to no one whom He does not, at the same time, humble in all things and bring into subjection to His vicar, the priest.

8. The penitential canons are imposed only on the living, and, according to them, nothing should be imposed on the dying.

9. Therefore the Holy Spirit in the pope is kind to us, because in his decrees he always makes exception of the article of death and of necessity.

10. Ignorant and wicked are the doings of those priests who, in the case of the dying, reserve canonical penances for purgatory.

11. This changing of the canonical penalty to the penalty of purgatory is quite evidently one of the tares that were sown while the bishops slept.

12. In former times the canonical penalties were imposed not after, but before absolution, as tests of true contrition.

13. The dying are freed by death from all penalties; they are already dead to canonical rules, and have a right to be released from them.

14. The imperfect health [of soul], that is to say, the imperfect love, of the dying brings with it, of necessity, great fear; and the smaller the love, the greater is the fear.

15. This fear and horror is sufficient of itself alone (to say nothing of other things) to constitute the penalty of purgatory, since it is very near to the horror of despair.

16. Hell, purgatory, and heaven seem to differ as do despair, almost-despair, and the assurance of safety.

17. With souls in purgatory it seems necessary that horror should grow less and love increase.

18. It seems unproved, either by reason or Scripture that they are outside the state of merit, that is to say, of increasing love.

19. Again, it seems unproved that they, or at least that all of them, are certain or assured of their own blessedness, though we may be quite certain of it.

20. Therefore by "full remission of all penalties" the pope means not actually "of all," but only of those imposed by himself.

21. Therefore those preachers of indulgences are in error, who say that by the pope's indulgences a man is freed from every penalty, and saved;

22. Whereas he remits to souls in purgatory no penalty which, according to the canons, they would have had to pay in this life.

23. If it is at all possible to grant to any one the remission of all penalties whatsoever, it is certain that this remission can be granted only to the most perfect, that is, to the very fewest.

24. It must needs be, therefore, that the greater part of the people are deceived by that indiscriminate and high-sounding promise of release from penalty.

25. The power which the pope has, in a general way, over purgatory, is just like the power which any bishop or curate has, in a special way, within his own diocese or parish.

26. The pope does well when he grants remission to souls [in purgatory], not by the power of the keys

(which he does not possess), but by way of intercession.

27. They preach man who say that so soon as the penny jingles into the money-box, the soul flies out [of purgatory].

28. It is certain that when the penny jingles into the money-box, gain and avarice can be increased, but the result of the intercession of the Church is in the power of God alone.

29. Who knows whether all the souls in purgatory wish to be bought out of it, as in the legend of Sts. Severinus and Paschal.

30. No one is sure that his own contrition is sincere; much less that he has attained full remission.

31. Rare as is the man that is truly penitent, so rare is also the man who truly buys indulgences, i.e., such men are most rare.

32. They will be condemned eternally, together with their teachers, who believe themselves sure of their salvation because they have letters of pardon.

33. Men must be on their guard against those who say that the pope's pardons are that inestimable gift of God by which man is reconciled to Him;

34. For these "graces of pardon" concern only the penalties of sacramental satisfaction, and these are appointed by man.

35. They preach no Christian doctrine who teach that contrition is not necessary in those who intend to buy souls out of purgatory or to buy confessionalia.

36. Every truly repentant Christian has a right to full remission of penalty and guilt, even without letters of pardon.

37. Every true Christian, whether living or dead, has part in all the blessings of Christ and the Church; and this is granted him by God, even without letters of pardon.

38. Nevertheless, the remission and participation [in the blessings of the Church] which are granted by the pope are in no way to be despised, for they are, as I have said, the declaration of divine remission.

39. It is most difficult, even for the very keenest theologians, at one and the same time to commend to the people the abundance of pardons and [the need of] true contrition.

40. True contrition seeks and loves penalties, but liberal pardons only relax penalties and cause them to be hated, or at least, furnish an occasion [for hating them].

41. Apostolic pardons are to be preached with caution, lest the people may falsely think them preferable to other good works of love.

42. Christians are to be taught that the pope does not intend the buying of pardons to be compared in any way to works of mercy.

43. Christians are to be taught that he who gives to the poor or lends to the needy does a better work than buying pardons;

44. Because love grows by works of love, and man becomes better; but by pardons man does not grow better, only more free from penalty.

45. 45. Christians are to be taught that he who sees a man in need, and passes him by, and gives [his money] for pardons, purchases not the indulgences of the pope, but the indignation of God.

46. Christians are to be taught that unless they have more than they need, they are bound to keep back what is necessary for their own families, and by no means to squander it on pardons.

47. Christians are to be taught that the buying of pardons is a matter of free will, and not of commandment.

48. Christians are to be taught that the pope, in granting pardons, needs, and therefore desires, their devout prayer for him more than the money they bring.

49. Christians are to be taught that the pope's pardons are useful, if they do not put their trust in them; but altogether harmful, if through them they lose their fear of God.

50. Christians are to be taught that if the pope knew the exactions of the pardon-preachers, he would rather that St. Peter's church should go to ashes, than that it should be built up with the skin, flesh and bones of his sheep.

51. Christians are to be taught that it would be the pope's wish, as it is his duty, to give of his own money to very many of those from whom certain hawkers of pardons cajole money, even though the church of St. Peter might have to be sold.

52. The assurance of salvation by letters of pardon is vain, even though the commissary, nay, even though the pope himself, were to stake his soul upon it.

53. They are enemies of Christ and of the pope, who bid the Word of God be altogether silent in some Churches, in order that pardons may be preached in others.

54. Injury is done the Word of God when, in the same sermon, an equal or a longer time is spent on pardons than on this Word.

55. It must be the intention of the pope that if pardons, which are a very small thing, are celebrated with one bell, with single processions and ceremonies, then the Gospel, which is the very greatest thing, should be preached with a hundred bells, a hundred processions, a hundred ceremonies.

56. The "treasures of the Church," out of which the pope. grants indulgences, are not sufficiently named or known among the people of Christ.

57. That they are not temporal treasures is certainly evident, for many of the vendors do not pour out such treasures so easily, but only gather them.

58. Nor are they the merits of Christ and the Saints, for even without the pope, these always work grace for the inner man, and the cross, death, and hell for the outward man.

59. St. Lawrence said that the treasures of the Church were the Church's poor, but he spoke according to the usage of the word in his own time.

60. Without rashness we say that the keys of the Church, given by Christ's merit, are that treasure;

61. For it is clear that for the remission of penalties and of reserved cases, the power of the pope is of itself sufficient.

62. The true treasure of the Church is the Most Holy Gospel of the glory and the gracc of God.

63. But this treasure is naturally most odious, for it makes the first to be last.

64. On the other hand, the treasure of indulgences is naturally most acceptable, for it makes the last to be first.

65. Therefore the treasures of the Gospel are nets with which they formerly were wont to fish for men of riches.

66. The treasures of the indulgences are nets with which they now fish for the riches of men.

67. The indulgences which the preachers cry as the "greatest graces" are known to be truly such, in so far as they promote gain.

68. Yet they are in truth the very smallest graces compared with the grace of God and the piety of the Cross.

69. Bishops and curates are bound to admit the commissaries of apostolic pardons, with all reverence.

70. But still more are they bound to strain all their eyes and attend with all their ears, lest these men preach their own dreams instead of the commission of the pope.

71. He who speaks against the truth of apostolic pardons, let him be anathema and accursed!

72. But he who guards against the lust and license of the pardon-preachers, let him be blessed!

73. The pope justly thunders against those who, by any art, contrive the injury of the traffic in pardons.

74. But much more does he intend to thunder against those who use the pretext of pardons to contrive the injury of holy love and truth.

75. To think the papal pardons so great that they could absolve a man even if he had committed an impossible sin and violated the Mother of God -- this is madness.

76. We say, on the contrary, that the papal pardons are not able to remove the very least of venial sins, so far as its guilt is concerned.

77. It is said that even St. Peter, if he were now Pope, could not bestow greater graces; this is blasphemy against St. Peter and against the pope.

78. We say, on the contrary, that even the present pope, and any pope at all, has greater graces at his disposal; to wit, the Gospel, powers, gifts of healing, etc., as it is written in I. Corinthians xii.

79. To say that the cross, emblazoned with the papal arms, which is set up [by the preachers of

indulgences], is of equal worth with the Cross of Christ, is blasphemy.

80. The bishops, curates and theologians who allow such talk to be spread among the people, will have an account to render.

81. This unbridled preaching of pardons makes it no easy matter, even for learned men, to rescue the reverence due to the pope from slander, or even from the shrewd questionings of the laity.

82. To wit: -- "Why docs not the pope empty purgatory, for the sake of holy love and of the dire need of the souls that are there, if he redeems an infinite number of souls for the sake of miserable money with which to build a Church? The former reasons would be most just; the latter is most trivial."

83. Again: -- "Why are mortuary and anniversary masses for the dead continued, and why does he not return or permit the withdrawal of the endowments founded on their behalf, since it is wrong to pray for the redeemed?"

84. Again: -- "What is this new piety of God and the pope, that for money they allow a man who is impious and their enemy to buy out of purgatory the pious soul of a friend of God, and do not rather, because of that pious and beloved soul's own need, free it for pure love's sake?"

85. Again: -- "Why are the penitential canons long since in actual fact and through disuse abrogated and dead, now satisfied by the granting of indulgences, as though they were still alive and in force?"

86. Again: -- "Why does not the pope, whose wealth is to-day greater than the riches of the richest, build just this one church of St. Peter with his own money, rather than with the money of poor believers?"

87. Again: -- "What is it that the pope remits, and what participation does he grant to those who, by perfect contrition, have a right to full remission and participation?"

88. Again: -- "What greater blessing could come to the Church than if the pope were to do a hundred times a day what he now does once, and bestow on every believer these remissions and participations?"

89. "Since the pope, by his pardons, seeks the salvation of souls rather than money, why does he suspend the indulgences and pardons granted heretofore, since these have equal efficacy?"

90. To repress these arguments and scruples of the laity by force alone, and not to resolve them by giving reasons, is to expose the Church and the pope to the ridicule of their enemies, and to make Christians unhappy.

91. If, therefore, pardons were preached according to the spirit and mind of the pope, all these doubts would be readily resolved; nay, they would not exist.

92. Away, then, with all those prophets who say to the people of Christ, "Peace, peace," and there is no peace!

93. Blessed be all those prophets who say to the people of Christ, "Cross, cross," and there is no cross!

94. Christians are to be exhorted that they be diligent in following Christ, their Head, through penalties, deaths, and hell;

95. And thus be confident of entering into heaven rather through many tribulations, than through the assurance of peace." [72]

Martin Luther's public outcry on church indulgence and the rapid circulation of his writings turned the people's discontent with the Roman Catholic Church into a raging inferno. The Church continued to send papal envoys to Luther to quiet him, but he moved further into a position defiant of the Pope.

By 1520, Luther's defiance of Rome was total. He believed by that time that Rome was actually the anti-Christ. At the end of 1520, Luther became even more defiant and publicly burned the papal bull that required his submission.[73] Martin Luther was supported by a variety of local German rulers. Some of them supported him for genuine religious beliefs, and some for genuine political reasons such as anything to lessen the power of the Pope. The common people eagerly accepted his ideas. This resulted in a real people's movement, and his theology was spread through Germany by numerous preachers.[74]

The rapid spread of his ideas was predominately because of the first known use of a "PR' campaign. Wittenberg court painter Lucas Cranach the Elder, a Luther supporter, employed a workshop (along with other workshops) to create multiple PR or propaganda images of Luther to get the message to the people and win over converts. Luther cooperated in this propaganda since accompanying biblical and religious messages highlighted his spiritual message.[75]

The public relations campaign was actually very sophisticated for the time. Different images and versions were depicted depending on what class or type of audience it was aimed at. For the intellectuals, Luther was portrayed as the learned professor with the doctor's beret. For the general masses, he was a German Hercules[76] beating down the dark forces of the religion, i.e. the Pope.

Along with this campaign, Luther's work in the translation of the Bible from Church Latin contributed greatly to a uniform written German language. For the first time ever, this allowed the common German people to read (if able to) the Bible for themselves. No longer did they need the priests of the Roman Catholic Church to interpret GODs writings for them. The monopoly and power of the Roman Catholic Church was seriously impacted.[77]

The good thing is that people were now able to read and attempt to understand the many meanings of the Bible, and derive from the Bible what they each need for their spiritual growth.

The bad thing is that, without the guidance and explanations of the Roman Catholic Church, some people came up with the interpretations of the Bible to 'suit'their situation and... let's say to have it mean what they wanted, not necessarily what our God wanted.

Eventually Church liturgy changed, and the decrees of rulers and cities gave the Reformation a firm organizational foundation through independent state churches. After decades of conflict, the Religious Peace of Augsburg granted freedom of worship to Protestants in 1555.[78]

| LUTHER AS MONK | LUTHER AS HERCULES | LUTHER AS PROFESSOR |

Protestant

Luther's ideas quickly became popular in Scandinavia, England, and the Netherlands. Protestantism eventually split into many more denominations as discussion and disputes arose over doctrine, theology, or religious practice. Lutherans and Reformed are two of these[79] branches.

Catholics and conservative Protestants agree on some major theological matters like the existence of angels, Mary's virgin conception, Jesus' sinless life, incarnation, crucifixion, bodily resurrection, the imminent return of Jesus to Earth in the second coming, Heaven, Hell, and the Trinity.

Perhaps the "five Solas" express the main difference between conservative Protestantism and Roman Catholicism. "*Sola*" means "*alone*" in Latin.

The first three Sola statements of the early Protestant movement stressed *Sola Scriptura*:" The Bible is the sole authority for Christian beliefs and practices. The Catholic Church stresses a balance between Biblical support and the tradition of the Church itself. "*Sola Gratia*:" One is saved through grace alone, given to the believer by God directly. The Catholic Church stresses the importance of church sacraments as a channel for God's grace. "*Sola Fide*:" Salvation is by the individual's faith alone in trusting Jesus Christ as Lord and Savior.[80]

The main differences are explained in this quote "...Evangelicals hold that the Catholic Church has gone beyond Scripture, adding teachings and practices that detract from or compromise the Gospel of God's saving grace in Christ.

Catholics, in turn, hold that such teaching and practices are grounded in Scripture and belong to the fullness of God's revelation. The Protestant rejection, Catholics say, results in a truncated and reduced understanding of the Christian reality."[81]

Lutheran

The Lutheran religion is named after Martin Luther (Page 25). Since he was originally a Roman Catholic Augustinian monk, there are many similarities in the Roman Catholic Church and the Lutheran church. Martin Luther kept the parts of the faith that were scriptural (based on the Bible).

Lutheranism is based on scripture alone. Roman Catholicism is based on scripture + Papal decrees + Church history. However, it could be said that the Lutheran denomination is closer to Catholicism than any other Protestant faith, and that this is because later reformers added more "interpretation" in their religious practices.

Luther preferred the designation "Evangelical", and today the usual title is "Evangelical Lutheran Church". In

Germany, Lutherans and the Reformed have been united since 1817. The term "Lutheran" is no longer used, and the state Church is called the Evangelical.[82]

Reformed Faith

The Protestant Reformation evolved into more than just the Lutheran denomination. Following behind Martin Luther, John Calvin added to the Evangelical faith by intensive studies into God's word. In 1536 he finished the first edition of the Institutes of the Christian Religion, where he explained in detail many doctrines in the Bible.

In fact, Luther and other founders of the faith agreed on much of this, but Calvin was the first to put these principles into a complete structure.[83] The Reformed Faith believes that the several branches of the visible church have misinterpreted the apostolic doctrines set forth in the Bible.[84] The Reformed faith holds that it is the closest approximation of what the Bible teaches. It was spoken in part by Augustine and was expressed fully in the teachings of John Calvin.

The Pilgrims and the Puritans held it to a greater or lesser degree. From a Reformed Faith viewpoint: "Every theology has a theme it revolves around. For example, Catholicism revolves around the universal church; Methodism revolves around sanctification; Pentecostalism revolves around the Holy Spirit; the Baptist faith revolves around the new birth; Lutheranism revolves around justification by faith; Greek Orthodoxy revolves around the Sacrament.

The Reformed faith, by contrast, revolves around God." [85] This Faith was also known as "Calvinism" and spread from Geneva, Switzerland into the rest of Europe.[86]

This Chapter covered the religions that my ancestors were probably part of over their thousands of years of development. The important idea to remember is not to evaluate the importance of religion in their lives using our present day standards. And almost everyone was eventually converted to Roman Catholic Christianity whether they wanted to or not.

These were times where the people still believed that if you were good that GOD would give you blessings, but if you were bad, then bad things happened. Daily life involved GOD, with their understanding controlled by the Roman Catholic Church interpretation. Church attendance was mandatory with punishment if you were a slacker.

Distribution of Religions 1618

Good people were still going to war over who was Catholic and who was Protestant. This is probably not the fault of the people or the religion, but was a result of the Roman Catholic Church becoming deeply involved in political affairs in government. Sounds far-fetched. Consider the deaths and destruction caused by the open warfare of the religious-political parties of Irish Protestants and Catholics in the 20th century. And in Germany, we are looking at a period 400 to 500 years earlier.

The old saying that "Politics and Religion should never mix" was true back then. Sadly, it is still very true even today.

Chapter II
The Büdingen Connection

Since Religion was such an important part of their lives, the soon-to-be German colonists could not just live together in Russia without the blessing of the Church. Those that signed up with the recruiters in Büdingen and were unmarried, took the opportunity to marry there. There was a also financial incentive from Catherine the Great for being a married emigrant couple. Büdingen Church records list 375 marriages of the future German colonists to Russia held from January through July of 1766. The lists are commonly called the Büdingen Marriage Lists, but were actually titled "Copuliert Russische Colonisten" or Married Russian Colonists.

Büdingen is located about 50N 9E about 24 miles northeast of Frankfurt am Main,[87] and is in a wet and swampy valley. The castle and the old town were built on centuries-old oak planks, which mean that the water level has to be kept high so no air can reach these foundations.[88]

Büdingen Woodcut 1624 [89]

The picture below is of the Marienkirche or Liebfrauenkirche in Büdingen. It has existed in one form or another since 1377 and was probably the church where the colonists married. At that time, it was Reformed Faith church. The Lutheran Church was built in 1769. The photo is from our time in Büdingen.

Marienkirche or Liebfrauenkirche in Büdingen

Chapter III
The First Hundred Years in the Volga Colonies

Three large religious groups settled in the Volga Colonies. The largest group by far was Lutheran with more than four thousand families. Next were the Catholics with around two thousand five hundred families. Third was the Reformed faith with about one thousand two hundred fifty families.[90] There were also a small number of families of the Orthodox Faith and the Mennonite Faith.[91]

The original plan may have been to settle villages according to religion as in Germany, and in some cases that did happen. Colony villages such as Anton, Balzer, Huck, Kutter, Messer, and Norka were of the Reformed faith according to the 1798 Census.

Bauer, Beideck, Dietel, Dönhof, Frank, Grimm, Hussenbach, Laub and Schilling were Lutheran. Brabander, Göbel, Graf, Herzog, Köhler, Mariental, Preuss, Schuck were Roman Catholic. Other villages such as Beuregard, Katharinenstadt, Lauwe, and Warenburg were a mixture of the three or four.[92] As the years went by, cross village marriages blurred the lines and mixed the religions even more.

While the Russian Government had promised to provide pastors, priests, and ministers for the Volga Colonies, they never lived up to it. During the period of 1764 to 1772, only seven Volga Colonies had pastors. By 1820, seventy-five

Protestant settlements had a total of 14 pastors. In 1860, there was only one minister for every 6,400 members.[93]

There were Protestant Pastors among the first Volga settlers that served their needs on the trip and accompanied them to their settlements. Several stand out in the historical records. The first was Lutheran Pastor Ludwig Balthasar Wernborner of Katharinenstadt who died in 1774 at the hands of the Kirghiz.

The second was Lutheran Pastor Laurentius Ahlbaum serving several Volga parishes thru 1786. The third was Reformed Pastor Johann Georg Herwig serving Katharinenstadt from 1767 -1769 and then Norka until his death in 1782. Fourth was another Reformed Pastor named Janet who served Anton from 1765 – 1771 and then Messer until 1803.

There were also Pastors Seeger of Beideck, Christian Tornow of Grimm from 1767 – 1781 and of Bettinger from 1781 – 1791, Mittelstadt of Frank, Bergen of Dietel, Ludwig Helm of Rosenheim from 1767 - 1785, and Pohlmann of Warenburg. Most of the Pastors only remained in the Volga Colonies for a short time.[94]

Catherine the Great (Sofia Augusta Fredrieka) was born into the Lutheran Faith. When she married the future Tsar Peter III, Sofia was baptized into the Russian Orthodox Church in 1774. At that time, she was given the name, Catherine Alexeyevna.

Whatever her name was, Sofia Augusta Fredrieka - Catherine Alexeyevna-Catherine the Great, her religious experience was as a Lutheran and as a Russian Orthodox.

Because of that, she was no great supporter of the Catholic colonists. Also, historical records tell us that the Russian Orthodox Church did not trust the religious and political maneuverings of the Pope in Rome.[95] In spite of those ideas, the Catholics did not suffer any more than the Protestants.

The historical records do show that there were Catholic Priests that accompanied the emigrating Catholic Germans to the Volga Colonies. One such priest, a Father Corbinian, a Capuchin of Melniza, Bohemia, accompanied a group of emigrants from Kassimow to their new homes on the Volga in 1767. While on the long and harsh trip, he ministered to all their spiritual needs. This included baptizing infants, blessing marriages, administering the sacraments and burying the many dead.

When the Catholic Colonies were founded, the first priests for Colonists were Franciscans and Capuchins. The nationality of these priests is unknown, but all could speak the German language fluently. All were greatly beloved by the people because of their deep spirituality and unassuming character. They were provided by the Russian government and most likely came from St. Petersburg, Libau or other cities of the Baltic provinces.

The Franciscans and Capuchins were followed by Dominicans and Trinitarians. They were also dedicated priests determined to support the people. Unfortunately for the Colonists, these men soon died off. Replacing them were Polish priests who as a rule were entirely ignorant of the German language with no understanding of German customs and manners.

Under their confusing ministering, the colonists lost much of their enthusiasm for Church religion. The situation became so bad that the settlers eventually complained to the government and demanded priests who could speak German. To quiet the Colonists, the Russian Government brought in ten Jesuits in 1803 that spoke German. The Polish priests were recalled back to Poland.

The Jesuits remained until they were banished in 1820. Under Jesuit guidance, the colonies underwent a religious new beginning. It was during this period that the foundations were laid of that lively faith, touching devotion, and whole-souled adherence to the Catholic Church. Unfortunately, the Jesuits were banished by the Government in the fall of 1820, and again replaced with Polish Regulars, Dominicans, Carmelites, Trinitarians, Vincentians and Lazarists. For some unknown reason, they ministered to their flocks in a very haphazard manner. Religious participation again declined. Eventually, German Catholic clergy replaced those that the people did not support.[96]

Church and School and Government and Customs and Traditions and Holidays and Celebrations were woven together to form their daily lives. There were no boundaries such as the separation of Church and State as we know in the United States. The idea of limiting Religion in their lives would have seemed to them as the idea of the insane, or worse, of the unbeliever.

Church and School

The Church played a substantial role in the Colonies progress and the Colonists daily life. It also provided a link back to old Germany. As mentioned above, there was always a shortage of trained Pastors. Many Pastors had three to six colonies in their parish ministering to a population of fifteen to twenty thousand. Even so, the various religions developed and organized public education long before any of the governments provided for it. The first total Russian census from the year 1897 listed that 76% of the Volga Germans were of the Lutheran Faith, 13.5% were of the Catholic Faith, 3.6% were of the Mennonite Faith, 1% were of some other Protestant Faith, and 0.75% were of the Orthodox Catholic Faith. More information on the religions of the Colonists is covered in a previous chapter.

The high point of the Religious week was always Sunday with the Sunday service being special in the church life of the colonies of the German-Russians. On Saturday, the people would end the week and would prepare for the special day by making sure the yard and road were swept. This insured that Sunday morning the entire family could go and/or drive to the church, and punctually arrive on time. And punctual attendance at Church was expected and required by Society. Of course, work on Sunday was strictly forbidden. The Church and Clergy was also a center point for Baptisms, Funerals, Weddings, Confirmations, and religious holidays. It also played a determining role in the retention and practice of the customs that were brought from the Old Country.

School was important for the continuation of the Colonies. Since the Russian Government was incapable or unwilling to provide education, the villages took it upon themselves to perform it. Remember that the colonies had been primarily assembled by religious faith, so that most were of one faith, i.e. Lutheran. So it was natural that the Church and local Government would also be of one faith, and that the school would be a "religious" school. The concept of "Separation of

Church and State" was not in favor at this time. Note that there were some villages that had more than one Church and Village sponsored school, i.e. one school for children of the Lutheran Faith and one school for children of the Reformed Faith.

The following is an example of Rules of Attendance for a Colony school in 1841:

SCHOOL ATTENDANCE (1841)

The following rules are prescribed for all village authorities, and all family fathers for the faithful observation and fulfilment of public education in these colonies:

§ 1. Each family father is obligated to send, and ensure their children, pupils, apprentices or a servant of both kinds of sex, from the seventh year, attend daily school and the Sundays Katechisation or child teachings, from the beginning of October to the end of March.

§ 2. Every schoolmaster will have a faithful roll call of all children obligated to attend school, and after completion both the morning and afternoon training hours, and also after each Katechisation or child teachings. The schoolmaster will present these roll calls of training attendance to the village authority of the colony each day.

§ 3. After he receives the roll calls, the village authority will note the missing pupils, and make inquiries with the families as to the causes of their missing classes. He will mark the records as to whether the absence was proper and therefore legal, or improper and without legal reason. Absences without legal reason will cause a fine,

determined by the family executive committee, to be assessed to the missing pupil's family father.

§ 4. Legal reasons of being missing from required attendance: Sickness of the pupil; the need to attend others of the family that are sick; a death in the family, however only up to the end of the funeral, and severe weather preventing safe travel to the school.

Note: Other legal reasons for missing required attendance can occur. The village authority, at their discretion, will judge whether these reasons are to be regarded as adequate for the release from the fine, or not.

§ 5. For each occurrence of a pupil missing from the school without a reason judged to be legal, the parents or guardians must pay 3 Crown silver to the family executive committee or village authority

§ 6. Any fines received by the village authority or the family executive committee for missing attendance will be added to the school cash.

§ 7. The school cash will be applied on an equal basis as determined by each Church Authority for the acquisition of required books for poor children, and for those books distributed with to the pupils distinguished by diligence.

§ 8. If the fine is not paid, or if the Village Authority judges the persons responsible unable to pay, then instead of the fine, the persons responsible will perform municipality work equal to each half-day the pupil missed school. [97]

Traditions, Customs, and Celebrations

The tradition of generations of families living together in one place in extended families was highly valued in the German Colonies. There was always plenty to be done, but there were always many to do it. There was a strict division of labor for men and women. The men worried about the agriculture and the cattle breeding; and the women concerned themselves with the house, kitchen, cellar, garden and the education of the children. Of course, when harvest came, it was all hands to the fields.

Parents had the unbroken authority over the children; family co-operation was remarkable. The grandmother (Grossmotter or Altmotter) and the female members of the families worried about the "soul life" of the children. They had the task teaching the children the "Gebotter" (the 10 requirements) to tell and thus pass on to their children. The grandmother also taught the children singing of the volks songs and music. She also taught the children Fairy tales to maintain a close connection to the old homeland for the German-Russians. Many Volga Colonies children knew Grimm's fairy tale just like the German children. Some of the details were changed to fit the Russian area, but the basic idea remained.

Along with the parents and grandparents, the village minister had great influence (as representative of the Church) to "say" how even private family life would run. He could put in a word about the education of the children, and was as expected a guardian over order, customs and morals of the family and children. As such, he would expect, and if necessary order, attendance at the Kirche service on Sunday. The Sunday Kirchgang was a firm component in the rhythm of the family life of the German-Russians.

For the Volga Germans, the fixed customs in the course of the year played an important role. Traditional celebrations and ceremonies that included Birth and child Baptism, Christmas, New Year, Three-King celebration, Fastnacht, Easter and Whitsuntide were celebrated.

Birth

The birth of a child, particularly the first born, was always a joyful event in the Colonies. A typical celebration is detailed in the following text: *"Taufstein-all next relatives, grandparents of the young citizen of the world, were particularly informed... of the lucky Niederkunft and birth and invited to the imminent child baptism. Usually the child, if it were healthy, was carried on the following Sunday to the holy baptism. Up to then one let the light burn in the whole house for the protection of the newborn child against bad spirit. The choice of the godfathers mostly depended on degrees of relationship, as the brothers and sisters of parents came first to the row. With the baptism the child usually got the name of the godfather, if womanlike - the names of the godmother. In former times one gave two and also three names to the children. If the godfathers were single, then the patin wore a white dress with the baptizing course and carried on the head a Kraenzchen. Sometimes the white Kleidchen of the Taeuflings - with a light blue or rosa volume around the Leibchen - and a silver or golden Kreuzchen was bought by the godfathers. As soon as the child was returned from the baptism by the godfathers and the midwife, the Taufschmaus began. It was eaten much and often drunk on the well being of the child and the nut/mother, who lay usually still in bed. A strange custom, probably taken by the Russians, took place during the meal. The midwife must have absolutely sweet liquor, otherwise one said, the child will not prosper. This liquor was prepared by the midwife with Branntwein and burned sugar and handed by it the godfathers and the other guests in a glass for costing. The guests nippten something at the glass, inserted a silver coin and passing on the same. Thus the glass moved with the sweet liquor to all guests and filled with coins into the hands of the midwife, as acknowledgment of its earnings/services with lucky relieving. In earlier times the child baptism were kept wasteful often quite solemnly and, so that from the welfare service committee strict prohibitions against the verschwendung and omittingness became to sometimes issue with child baptism and weddings of the Kolonisten."*

Christmas

Christmas was celebrated in the Volga Colonies according to old homeland custom. The celebration took three days. Afterwards they celebrated New Year, and in the Colonies of Catholic Faith, the celebration of the Holy Three Kings. A typical celebration is detailed in the following text: *"at the Christmas eve in the praying hall a Christmas tree deseamed with candles and glass decoration was set up. Under this tree baskets with Naschereien were such as sweets, apples and walnuesse. Also at home Christmas trees were set up. Since it was difficult depending upon location of the colony to procure fir trees also different branches of tree had to hold as replacement. First the common Christian celebration of the municipality in the praying hall took place. After sunset and that blade of the first bell ring met all there. The following second bell ring ended only after singing first Chorals by the municipality. Afterwards the larger school boys, who had procured a ringing, came also into the praying hall. One sang Christmas carols common. Before the prayer, the child choir "silence sang night, holy night" to telling the Weihnachtsgeschichte and a following short devotion. The texts of the old will with the prophecies of the birth Jesus* were brought in the form of questions and answers of the pupils in memory. Between them one sang Christmas carols. After this ceremony the men seized the baskets with the Naschereien and did not distribute contents to yet the schoolable children In the connection a short prayer took place and after the singing of the song "Oh, you merry..." made itself the municipality of glad courage on the way home. There then actual giving began; those was predominantly limited to apples, Naschereien and clothes. Christmas carols were likewise sung. At families with smaller children the Christian child appeared for giving. Also Santa Claus was already well-known in some areas. In order old persons and patients, who could not participate in the celebration of the municipality to make a joy the Christian eight-singing was far common. Some municipality members met before the house of the persons concerned and pleased them with a Staendchen. At the Christmas Eve one went late to bed. The following holidays were used for utilization and acquaintance attendance. One was partly guest, partly hosts."

New Year

A typical celebration is detailed in the following text:*"that was a life in the colonies, if at the New Year the small Buben and girls its" Pedder "and" Geddel " (godfather) anwuenschten" s'Neujohr "and richly presented diverted with Bretzeln, lebkuchen, apples and Nuessen again returned home. The usual congratulations on the New Year with the small ones read: "Pedder and Geddel I wish ' you e luck-blessed, new Johr, health, long life and the eternal luck blessedness."As the small ones its godfather the New Year anwuenschten, then became of the adult male youth, particularly the large Buben, their godfather, grandparents and the girls (humans) the New Year angeschossen. With a loaded pistol or gun Bur came to the window, knocked and* called: "Pedder and Geddel I wish ' you e luck-blessedly new Johr!", then: "Buff, buff", so that all windowpanes trembled. Soon the Tuere opened and the Schiesser into the room was invited, with wine or liquor and cake regaled. If it received then still another gift, it left again secretly the house, in order not of is awake to be gotten and into the Brummer set. Despite the many accidents and the strict police prohibition shooting at New Year in many colonies kept for a long time. In another place met the single youth up to 6 January each evening in a house to the dance. In addition the young men organized gallop running on the main street of the village. On the last day of the yearly appeared with much polarizing so-called fur nickel (a legend shape originating from the Elsass). That was one with sheep fur, Zottelmuetze and mask disguised person, who distributed blows to unartige children. (in some municipalities however also the Christian child as well as fur nickel appeared).Briefly before midnight the church-bells rang the old year out. Now the new year was likewise received with bell ringing; often connected with services."

Three Kings Celebration

In the Colonies of the Catholic Faith, the custom of the Three King Day was for three boys of ages eleven to thirteen, dressed in white shirts and with a decorated kronartigen cap, to go from house to house in the village singing the following song (note that the translation is a little rough):

Three kings lead by the light of GOD

I.

**With a star from morning country everything - Alleluja
To the Christian child near Jerusalem
In a stable to Betlehem, Everything - Alleluja.**

Where it is holy, his name is called: Jesus Christ
And because of our wealth, of the sky came ,
Everything - Alleluja.

The star, and te way we must go. We want the go day still further, Everything - Alleluja.

You gave ' us a gift, The year are to live you with joys, Probably, you and your children! Probably you and your children!

II.

Three kings of God hand lead by a star from morning country,
To the Christian child near Jerusalem, Into a stable of Bethlehem.
Refrain: All, everything, Alleluja!

We are traveled in faster let us hurry '
In thirteen day ' four hundred mile ',
Uphill, downhill by snow and ice,
We finished the long race '.

Refrain

The star and the way we must go, We want to go the day still further.

Come their pointing! to Jesus alone in the crib,
Carry the ways the victim to Jesus so tenderly:
Because this frightened us and up-aroused us from the sleep.
Come the Angels! to the beautiful child alone in the crib.

Come their pointing! to Jesus in the crib all alone,
Carry the ways the victim to Jesus Lord,
Because he is our God, he will protect us in dire times,
Come here all! to the beautiful child alone in the crib.

**Come their pointing, with ointments and anoint the child!
Contribute the ways beautiful child of Maria to it.
Fall down one hundred times, fall down thousands times!
Arose Jesus Christ, who is truly born.**

Easter

The Easter of the Colonies began with the Karfreitag (Charfreitag). This was a day of remembering the death of Christ. On this day the "adults" were not allowed to eat anything. On the Charfreitag/Charwoche (Karwoche), everyone would be busy and working in the colonies. The women of the colony would be extremely busy. At Easter everything had to be clean in the house and yard, and food brought and prepared for the different celebration table settings.

The most important people during this time were the Raetschebuwe. After the church service, the bells were silent, and were only rung on Saturday again. The Raetschebuwe provided to the village what the bells normally did. The Raetschebuwe were usually the oldest pupils of the Pfarrschule. They made sure that everyone had Raet, a wooden instrument provided with a crank, which made a sharp clack when turned rapidly. The Raetschebuwe positioned themselves on all the different lanes of the village; and at the same time all turned their Raet, which resulted in a large noise. After they had turned their Raets for about 5 minutes, the leader would raise his Raet to stop all the others.

They would sing this in the morning:

> "the day begins to brighten
> The arms like the realms.
> Ave Maria, *full of grace!*"

They would sing this at noon:
> "your Leut ', their Leut ', which we want to say you!
> The Bell *struck* twelve.
> Ave Maria, *full of grace!*"

They would sing this in the evening:
> "your Leut ', their Leut ', s ' is Betglockzeit!
> Ave *Maria* , full of grace!"

They would sing this to invite into the church:
> *" It is first (or second , the latter)*
> *Times in D ' Kirch."*

For doing this work the Raetschebuwe would go house to house with a basket for donations, and singing:
> *"we have talked over the holy grave,*
> *Thus give us also one eastresulted in!*
> *Not so largely and not so small,*
> *That are in's Koerbele no."*
> *If they receive then a gift (eggs or money), they sang:*
> *"that is the all-most beautiful house,*
> *Do look three angels to the window out."*

Note that this custom is still performed in Germany. We were able to enjoy observing it while we lived in rural Hoppachshof, Germany. It did take us a while to understand why all these young people were running around with these wooden clackers making noise and then singing… Remember, the village bells do not ring during this time, so in the old days (before personal time pieces) the only way to know the hour at this holiday was the hourly Raetschebuwe performance.

The Ostersonntag/Easter Sunday would begin at sunrise with a Choral, which was blown by the trombone choir and/or sung by the singer choir. The village people would meet early at the village Church. From the Church they would all walk together to the village cemetery and sing Auferstehungs or Osterlieder. A speech would be given, and afterwards each person would visit the graves of their relatives to pray. After they had visited all of the graves, they would return to their homes and prepare for the Easter service held in the church.

Just as happens today on Ostersonntag, before the young children wake, colored eggs were hidden for the children to find. The idea was the same, to gather as many eggs as possible. Some games that the children played among themselves made some children winners of even more eggs from the other children that lost their eggs. One such game was the "Eierschurwle."

In this game, a brettchen (broetchen-hard long bread) was placed in incline against a wall with a group of eggs laid out in a semi-circle at the bottom of the broetchen. An egg was rolled down the bread and if it stopped next to one of the eggs already in the semi-circle, both eggs belonged to the player (kind of like playing marbles, except that eggs roll erratically).

Ascension Day

The Ascension Day celebration was a high point for the people. The Ascension is one of the great feasts in Christianity, and commemorates the bodily Ascension of Jesus into Heaven forty days after his resurrection from the dead. A service at the friedhof or cemetery would take took place in the afternoon before the town celebration.

The Pfingstfest

The Pfingstfest was one of the main celebrations for the Volga Germans. The Pfingstfest is 50 days past Easter. The previous evening and the whole night the colonies would sing.

Whitsuntide

Whitsuntide is the celebration of the Holy Spirit and forms the conclusion of the Easter circle in the church year. At Whitsuntide, the Confirmation ceremony also took place. Friends from other areas would come to attend the Confirmation. Choirs and other groups visited and sang two songs for friends, the minister, the schulmeister (school master), and at the house of the person to be confirmed.

Weddings

As still happens today, Weddings were ruled by Custom handed down over the years. The advertisement of the bride (request for her hand) usually took place after midnight with a representative of the bridegroom loudly knocking on the house door. After (and if) the groom's representative was allowed in by the prospective bride's father, the groom's proposal would be carefully (and respectfully) offered.

Depending upon how the father felt about the proposal, the father would put out the light and go to bed (no), or accepted the proposal with wine. If yes, the future bridegroom, the future bride and her mother were called. The bride received a small gift, usually handkerchiefs. The bride would promise to sew the wedding shirt for the groom. This private engagement was continued with liquor and a lunch. The public and church engagement took place on the next day, usually Saturday. Before the announcement, the minister would test their knowledge of the Christian teachings. Only after a successful examination would the public engagement take place.

After successful bride advertisement and public or church engagement announcement, the wedding could be prepared. In the Volga area weddings were normally held in the Spring. The invitation of the wedding guests took place in accordance with ritual. The actual wedding took place usually on a weekday. The grooms' family invited single wedding guests personally to a celebration on the Sunday before the actual Wedding Day.

Two days before the Wedding Day, invitations were presented to the other guests. The bride and its parents were the first persons, who received an invitation. The invitation was spoken. The meeting of the guests on the wedding day took place separately.

The guests of the groom fetched the "bride" from her parents' house. Custom set down that a fake bride would be shown to the wedding company first (wrong brides- old, thick), who were rejected or "entruestet".

The real bride (already in the bride dress - usually dark-blue or light blue, sometimes also black, with artificial flowers and a white veil reaching up to the ground) was tied up with small bands to a chair, and had to be searched for by the grooms' guests and released from her bonds. Once she was found and released, the Wedding ritual could proceed.

The procession to the Wedding House was in the following order: In front were the two announcers with their wedding sticks. Following them were musicians, then the Bride with her maids, the Groom with two of his Godfathers, the guests, the Bride and Groom's parents, and finally, the "Schiesser" who fired shots into the air.

In the wedding house, all were celebrated. After the wedding house celebration, all walked to the church. The walking group was accompanied by the ring of the church-bells and the music of the musicians. In the church the wedding took place following the religious custom and ritual.

The groom made his way home before the wedding party. At the home, everyone got ready for the wedding meal. The groom, however, would not be present. The meal would begin with a table prayer. Following tradition, since the groom was not present, the bride would refuse all offers of food. Everyone else enjoyed the meal. After the meal was over and finished, the groom would arrive and "kidnap" his bride and take her to a separate private area to share their first meal together.

Meanwhile the common area was transformed for dancing. The dance was opened, in which the bridal pair first danced alone. Afterwards the pair requested in sequence the godfathers, the bride leaders, and bridesmaids. After this "bride row" the older youth danced. Dancing such as the Polka lasted till after midnight. Eventually, the groom led his bride to the wedding bed that the
older women had prepared.

The actual wedding day belonged to the youth with the old remaining in the background. The old ones sat in an adjoining room and sang volkslieder (people songs), told anecdotes or politisierten (politics). The day after belonged however to the old ones. It had the character of a carnival with dancing, singing, and punch drinking.

Wedding gifts were officially prohibited "until debts to the state are paid."[98] This was in keeping with the idea that all monies were to be repaid to the government. Newlyweds were required to plant twenty trees in honor of their wedding. Later if they had a son, they were required to plant six trees, and if a daughter, four trees.[99]

Funerals

The life span of the German-Russians was usually 60 to 70 years. If someone felt that his last hour was approaching, he would ask for a white-covered table on which two leuchter and a Bible and/or a gesangbuch to be placed beside his bed. Trauemde- take parting from the deceased.The dying received the communion.

In the hour of death, all the family was present if possible. One said quiet prayers and cried parting tears. After death, the passing was made public. As soon as the relatives were informed, they would come into the house of the deceased, kneel down and pray for the soul and peace of the deceased.

On the third day, the deceased was buried after funeral ceremony. The grave would be marked with crosses made from wood or iron. After the ceremony, a funeral lunch or a mourning meal would be held with all the relatives and friends attending. Days later, on the seventh and thirtieth day, relatives would also meet in a ceremony for the deceased.

The Kirchweihe

The Kirchweihe celebration is a church "lay" harvest thanks celebration. It was celebrated in the autumn. Around this time, the bounty of the pastures and land came, and from those sales the village received money and material assets. The celebration was an expression of unrestrained life and good times. The villagers began 14 days before the celebration with the preparations. Foods were baked and roasted. On the specified Sunday, the celebration would begin and continue over two days.

The celebration consisted of dancing and drinking and partying. The consequences were frequent fights and illegitimate children. The church did not approve of this celebration and regularly preached against it, however the villagers still enjoyed it.

Note that the Kirchweihe celebration is still happening in Germany. We were lucky enough to be invited to many village Kirchweihe where we met many people, sang many songs, and enjoyed much German beer. We did not see any fighting.

What we did see was many happy people enjoying being with their friends and neighbors. Maybe the Church just felt that having fun was anti-religious..

Chapter IV
Churches of the Volga Colonies

Over the years, I thought of my German-Russian ancestors as being poor simple farmers. That was so wrong. While it may have been true at the start of the colonies, by the late 1800's they had a sophisticated society. They were able to build many beautiful Houses of Worship while they lived there. The following pages of beautiful churches they built prove that they were much more than just the poor simple farmers.

The first churches in the area were built shortly after the founding of the colonies. These early churches were simple wooden structures built quickly. With more emigrants arriving and a growing population rate, they were soon replaced. Remember, this was a time when everyone went to church. If you did not go for your soul, then you went for the good of the society. For those that chose not to participate, society had Laws to punish or correct their attitudes. Historical records show that if a person chose not go to Church, the village authorities could, and at times did, banish them from the village.

In 1800, new churches began to be constructed. In the ten years from 1820 to 1830, over twenty-five new wood churches were constructed. Construction techniques became better and the wood was replaced with brick. By 1885, there were 83 Lutheran and 27 Catholic Churches in the Volga Colonies. Over time, a type of Volga German Church architecture evolved with characteristics of very tall pointed bell towers, curving windows and arches, with colorfully decorated tile walls. The builders view was that the church must be the most important and beautiful building in the village.[100]

Only a handful of these churches exist today. Most are in horrible condition. Each time that the Russian Government outlawed religion, the churches would be damaged or destroyed. Of course, when Stalin finally "permanently" removed the German-Russians, most traces of the churches were eradicated. The lucky buildings that survived were modified and used as warehouses, grainaries, or schools. Some were left to rot in the weather. Katherinenstadt and Warenburg met this sad end.

Balzer Church [101]

Dinkel Church [102]

Frank Church [103]

Grimm Church

Herzog Church

Katherinenstadt Church [104]

Katherinenstadt Church in 1997 [105]

Obermunjou Catholic Church

Saratov Evangelical Church [106]

Schwed Lutheran Church

Straub Church [107]

Shcherbakovka Church [108]

Yagodnaya Polyana Church [109]

Yost Church [110]

Warenburg Church [111]

Warenburg Church in 2003 [112]

Warenburg Church Interior [113]

Warenburg Church Interior in 2003 [114]

Chapter V
All Things Must Change

The intertwining of Religion in their daily lives stayed much the same for 100 years. Rulers and policies changed in Moscow and in 1861, Russian Tsar Alexander II emancipated and gave all the serfs equal status with the Volga Germans. The "privileges" that Catherine the Great granted had ended. In 1871, the Colonies right to self-government was ended with the nullification of the colonial law that granted it. Religious freedom was attacked with laws prohibiting ownership of land unless they converted to the Orthodox Faith.[115]

In 1892, Alexander III outlawed land acquisition by non-Orthodox citizens in the west. To land-starved colonists who had helped found many new colonies and who had plans to start more, this policy seemed to aim directly at their freedom of religion, which Catherine had also guaranteed.[116]

Many realized their religious freedom was at risk. They decided that to be their Faith was more important to them than any loyalty to the Volga Colonies, and they emigrated away from the Volga. From 1874 to 1890, it is estimated that 30,000 Germans left Russia for the freedoms of the Americas.[117]

With the beginning of the First World War, the situation for the German-Russians suddenly became even worse. The Tsars' Russian government adopted two laws in 1915. They were called "liquidation laws", because both aimed at the base of life of the German settlers, the ownership of land.

The first law determined, that all persons of German, Austrian and Hungarian nationality, who had become Russian citizens after 1 January 1880 in a zone of 150 Werst along the border to Germany and Austria Hungary as well as in a zone of 100 Werst along the coast of Baltic Sea, Black Sea, and Asov Sea, must sell their land their landed property within ten to sixteen months to someone still eligible to own property. Persons that were of the Orthodox Faith or those that renounced their religion and switched to the Orthodox Faith were able to keep their land and own even more.

The Bolshevik Revolution and violent civil war ended enforcement of the 1915 laws. However, the new Russian provisional government also supported only the Orthodox Faith. The provisional government quickly fell, and the Communists gained control.

The Communist Government of Lenin was one of devastation and death. His "subculture of massacre" affected all Russia, and the Volga area did not escape. While Lenin did not personally order execution or mass murder, he did install and use the Soviet system of terror.[118]

By 1919, all pastors were arrested as counter revolutionary propagandists and were sent to slave camps.[119] Any Religion, even the Orthodox Faith, would now have to remain hidden.

That did not stop the practice of their religious faiths; it just moved it out of the public view. Church services were in private homes. As all the ministers, pastors, and priests had been rounded up and sent to correction camps, the services were led by "Betenbrüder" or "praying brethren." These were lay members that would preside over the prayer meetings. This had been a practice since the early days of start of the Volga Colonies, but it became much more important with the removal of the ministers and priests.[120]

Lenin's heir, Stalin just made the practice of their religion more difficult. Stalin and the Communist Government were not through with them yet. The end of the German-Russians and their Volga Colonies was only a handful of years in the future.

That story continues in another of my books:

"Moscow's Final Solution: The Genocide of the German-Russian Volga Colonies"

Summary

Religion and church were important foundations of the daily structure of the Volga German-Russians lives. Maybe it was the belief in a power or powers beyond themselves.[121] Or maybe it was the personal connection with the Superior power or powers overseeing the world. For whatever reasons, the Volga German-Russians overcame tremendous setbacks and still prospered and multiplied. I can only guess that it was some inner strength that did not allow them to quit. Did that inner strength come from their genetic DNA, their Germanic cultures, or their strong religious backgrounds? There is no way to tell the most important. Their strong religious faith was as important as either of the other two.

Forgotten Volga German Grave & Tombstone in Warenburg Cemetery 2003 [122]

We cannot forget all they did for us.

D. Philipp Kaiser - 2006

Bibliography

80th Anniversary Of The Free Evangelical Lutheran Cross Church 1892-1972, (Fresno, California, 1972)

Apocalypse, <http://www.pbs.org/wgbh/pages/frontline/shows/apocalypse/art/pic_indulgence.jpg>, accessed 9 April 2006

Avignon Papacy, <http://en.wikipedia.org/wiki/Avignon_papacy>, accessed 11 April 2006

Avignon Papal Place, <http://crusades.boisestate.edu/vpilgrim/images/France/Avignon/PapalPalace.jpg>, accessed 11 April 2006

Bach, Marcus, *Major Religions of the World*, (Nashville: Abingdon Press, 1977)

Barrett, David et al, *World Christian Encyclopedia: A comparative survey of churches and religions - AD 30 to 2200,*(Oxford University Press, 2001)

Benjes, C., *Geschichtsbilder*, (Wilhelm Susserott, Berlin, 1902)

Bilder Deutscher Geschichte, (O.H.W.Hadank, Berlin, 1936)

Cavendish, Richard, *The Great Religions*, (New York, Arco Publishing, Inc; 1980)

Cellar, Konrad, *The German colonies in South Russia*, (Historical Research Association of the Germans from Russia, Stuttgart, Munich 2000): pp. 110-111

Celts, <http://glossary.cassiopaea.com/glossary.php?id=898&lsel=C>, accessed 11 April 2006

Charlemagne, <http://en.wikipedia.org/wiki/Charlemagne>, accessed 10 April 2006

Comparing the Beliefs of Roman Catholics and Conservative Protestants, <http://www.religioustolerance.org/chr_capr.htm>, accessed 16 June 2005

Eastern Orthodox Church, <http://en.wikipedia.org/wiki/Eastern_Orthodox>, accessed 9 April 2006

Ecumenical and Schismatic Movements in Christianity, <http://www.religioustolerance.org/chr_ecdi.htm>, accessed 15 June 2005

Fouracre, Paul, *Frankish Gaul to 814*, (The new Cambridge Medieval History, Vol 2, Cambridge, 1995)

Fournier, K.A. & Watkins, W.D., *A House United*, (Navpress, Colorado Springs, CO, 1994)

Gaer, Joseph, *What the Great Religions Believe*, (New York, Dodd, Mead & Company, 1963)

Geisinger, Adam, *From Catherine to Krushchev: The Story of Russia's Germans* (Winnipeg, Canada; Marian Press, 1974)

Gnostic Christianity, <http://www.thepearl.org/What_is_Gnosticism.htm>, accessed 10 April 2006

Gutsche, Horst W., *Katherinenstadt Church in 1997*, http://www.members.cox.net/russland/Volga.pdf, accessed 20 June 2006

Hadas, Moses, *Imperial Rome*, (Time Inc, New York, 1965)

Harms, Wilmer A., *Insights Into Russia,* (Journal of the AHSGR, Lincoln, NE, Volume 26, No. 2 Spring 2003)

Haynes, Emma S., *A History of the Volga Relief Society*, (AHSGR, Lincoln, NE, 1982)

Henotheism, <http://en.wikipedia.org/wiki/Henotheism>, accessed 11 April 2006

History, <http://web.quipo.it/minola/frysk/history_of_the_frisian_people.htm> accessed 8 April 2006

History of Christianity, <http://www.mnsu.edu/emuseum/cultural/religion/christianity/history.html>, accessed 8 April 2006

Hoffman, Stefanie, *From Puppets of Stalin to Pawns of Hitler & Back Again: Experiences of Soviet Citizens of German Ethnicity During & After the Second World War*, (Journal of the AHSGR, Lincoln, NE, Volume 28, No. 1 Spring 2005)

Hooker, Richard, *The Celts*, <http://www.wsu.edu:8080/~dee/MA/CELTS.HTM>, accessed 8 April 2006

Hume, Robert E., *The World's Living Religions*, (New York, Charles Scribner's Sons, rev.ed.1959)

Introduction, <http://www.opc.org/what_is/Reformed_intro.html#Int1>, accessed 15 May 2005

Jewish Christianity, <http://philtar.ucsm.ac.uk/encyclopedia/judaism/messiah.html>, accessed 9 April 2006

Jones,Terry H., *Saint Boniface*

Lehmann, Arthur C. & James E. Myers, Magic, *Witchcraft, and Religion: An Anthropological Study of the Supernatural,*(Mountain View, California: Mayfield Publishing Company, 1993)

"Liudolfing" Dukes of Saxony, Kings of Germany, <http://home.wxs.nl/~voort359/home3liudf.html>, accessed 11 April 2006

Lutheranism, <http://www.newadvent.org/cathen/09458a.htm>, accessed 12 April 2006

Mai, Brent Allan, *1798 Census of the German Colonies along the Volga,* Vol 1 & 2, (AHSGR, Lincoln, NE, 1999)

Martin Luther – Times, <http://www.luther.de/en/kontext/>, accessed 11 April 2006

Merian, Matthew, *Büdingen,* Woodcut 1624

O'Brien, John A. Rev, *the faith of millions,* (Our Sunday Visitor, Inc, Huntington, In. 1963)

Ozment, Steven, *A Mighty Fortress*; *A New History of the German People,* (New York, NY, HarperCollins, 2004)

Pauline Christianity, <http://en.wikipedia.org/wiki/Pauline_Christianity>, accessed 11 April 2006

Pisarevskii, G.G., "*Internal Order in the Volga Colonies under Catherine II,*"(Warsaw, 1914): p. XVI

Pleve, Igor, *Einwanderung in das Wolgagebiet 1764-1767,* Vol 1,(Der Göttingen Arbeitskreis, 37085 Gottingen, 1999)

Polytheism, <http://en.wikipedia.org/wiki/Polytheism>, accessed 11 April 2006

Reformed, <http://www.tulip.org/ccr/reformed.htm>, accessed 11 April 2006

Religion, http://skyways.lib.ks.us/genweb/archives/ethnic/german-russian/jubilee/religion.shtml, accessed 20 June 2006

Religions of the World, <http://www.mnsu.edu/emuseum/cultural/religion/>, accessed 9 April 2006

Religious Tolerance, <http://www.religioustolerance.org/rcc_othe.htm>, accessed 11 April 2006

Roman Catholic Church, <http://en.wikipedia.org/wiki/Roman_Catholic>, accessed 9 April 2006

Roman Catholicism, <http://www.rapidnet.com/~jbeard/bdm/Cults/Catholicism/catholic.htm>, accessed 11 April 2006

Roman Religion, <http://www.unrv.com/culture/roman-religion.php>, accessed 12 April 2006

Sandlin, Andrew, *Survey of Reformed Faith*, <http://www.vidaeterna.org/eng/bible_studies/reformed_faith.htm>, accessed 12 April 2006

Scherbakovka Church, http://www.webbitt.com/volga/lower/shcherbakovka.html, accessed 20 June 2006

Scribner, RW, *For the Sake of the Simple Folk: Popular Propaganda for the German Reformation*, (Cambridge, 1981)

Shamanism, <http://en.wikipedia.org/wiki/Shamanism>, accessed 11 April 2006

Shelley, Fred M. and Audrey E. Clarke, *Human and Cultural Geography* (Dubuque, Iowa: Wm. C. Brown Publishers, 1994)

Spaeth, Adolph, Reed, L.D., Jacobs, Henry Eyster, et Al., Trans. & Eds., *95 Thesis*, (Philadelphia: A. J. Holman Company, 1915): Vol.1

The Jesus Movements, <http://www.religioustolerance.org/chr_hisb.htm>, accessed 15 August 2005

The Other Reichs, <http://europeanhistory.about.com/cs/germany/a/Otherreichs.htm>, accessed 15 August 2005

The Protestant Reformation,
<http://www.newgenevacenter.org/west/reformation.htm>, accessed 22 March 2005

The Reformation in Germany,
<http://www.loc.gov/exhibits/dres/dres3.html>, accessed 10 April 2006

The Religion of the Ancient Celts, <http://www.sacred-texts.com/neu/celt/rac/rac04.htm>, accessed 9 April 2006

The Role of Churches in Germany,
http://www.goethe.de/ges/rel/dos/en113534.htm, accessed 20 June 2006

Warnke, Martin, *Cranach's Luther*. Entwürfe für ein Image (Frankfurt: Fischer Taschenbuch Verlag, 1984)

White, Sharon, *German Tombstone in Warenburg Cemetery in 2003*

White, Sharon, *Warenburg Church 2003*

Williams, Hattie Plum, *The Czar's Germans*, (AHSGR, Lincoln, NE, 1975)

Wucher, Albert, *Illustrierte Weltgeschichte*, (Linden Verlag, Koln, 1982)

End Notes

[1] *The Role of Churches in Germany*
[2] Gaer, Joseph, *What the Great Religions Believe*, p.16
[3] Cavendish, Richard, *The Great Religions*, p.2
[4] *Religions of the World*
[5] Hume, Robert E., *The World's Living Religions*, p. 3
[6] Bach, Marcus, *Major Religions of the World*, p. 12
[7] *Polytheism*
[8] *The Religion of the Ancient Celts*
[9] Hooker, Richard, *The Celts*

[10] *Celts*
[11] *The Religion of the Ancient Celts*
[12] Hooker, Richard, *The Celts*
[13] *Celts*
[14] *The Religion of the Ancient Celts*
[15] Hooker, Richard, *The Celts*
[16] *The Religion of the Ancient Celts*
[17] Hooker, Richard, *The Celts*
[18] *History*
[19] Shelley, Fred M. and Audrey E. Clarke, *Human and Cultural Geography*
[20] Lehmann, Arthur C. & James E. Myers, Magic, *Witchcraft, and Religion: An Anthropological Study*
[21] *Shamanism*
[22] *Henotheism*
[23] *Roman Religion*
[24] ibid
[25] *Roman Catholicism*
[26] Barrett, David et al, *World Christian Encyclopedia: A comparative survey of churches and religions*
[27] *History of Christianity*
[28] *Ecumenical and Schismatic Movements in Christianity*
[29] Shelley, Fred M. and Audrey E. Clarke, eds. *Human and Cultural Geography*
[30] *Ecumenical and Schismatic Movements in Christianity*
[31] *Religious Tolerance*
[32] *Jewish Christianity*
[33] *The Jesus Movements*
[34] *Gnostic Christianity*
[35] Hadas, Moses, *Imperial Rome*
[36] *Pauline Christianity*
[37] *Religious Tolerance*
[38] O'Brien, John A. Rev, *the faith of millions*, p. 111
[39] *History of Christianity*

40 O'Brien, John A. Rev, *the faith of millions*, p. 22
41 *Roman Catholic Church*
42 Wucher, Albert, *Illustrierte Weltgeschichte*, pp. 232-233
43 ibid
44 Benjes, C., *Geschichtsbilder*, p.18
45 ibid, p. 17
46 Jones, Terry H., *Saint Boniface*
47 Unknown Artist
48 Ozment, Steven, *A Mighty Fortress; A New History of the German People*, p. 39
49 Benjes, C., *Geschichtsbilder*, pp. 19-23
50 *Bilder Deutscher Geschichte*, p. 7
51 Unknown Artist
52 Fouracre, Paul, *Frankish Gaul to 814*, pp. 102-103
53 *"Liudolfing" Dukes of Saxony, Kings of Germany*
54 Unknown Artist
55 Fouracre, Paul, *Frankish Gaul to 814*, pp. 102-103
56 Wucher, Albert, *Illustrierte Weltgeschichte*, pp. 235-236
57 Unknown Artist
58 *"Liudolfing" Dukes of Saxony, Kings of Germany*
59 Ozment, Steven, *A Mighty Fortress; A New History of the German People*, p. 41
60 *Charlemagne*
61 Wucher, Albert, *Illustrierte Weltgeschichte*, p. 238
62 *The Other Reichs*
63 Wucher, Albert, *Illustrierte Weltgeschichte*, pp. 348-349
64 *Avignon Papacy*
65 *Avignon Papal Place*
66 *Eastern Orthodox Church*
67 *Martin Luther – Times*
68 *Apocalypse*
69 Author created
70 O'Brien, John A. Rev, *the faith of millions*, pp. 194-202
71 *The Protestant Reformation*

[72] Spaeth, Adolph, Reed, LD, Jacobs, Henry Eyster, et Al., Trans.
& Eds., *95 Thesis*, pp. 29-38
[73] *The Protestant Reformation*
[74] *The Reformation in Germany*
[75] Warnke, Martin, *Cranach's Luther*. Entwürfe für ein Image, p. 65
[76] Scribner, RW, *For the Sake of the Simple Folk*, pp. 14-34
[77] *Martin Luther – Times*
[78] *The Reformation in Germany*
[79] *History of Christianity*
[80] *Comparing the Beliefs of Roman Catholics and Conservative Protestants*
[81] Fournier, K. A. & Watkins, W.D., *A House United*, pp. 337-349
[82] *Lutheranism*
[83] *Reformed*
[84] *Introduction*
[85] Sandlin, Andrew, *Survey of Reformed Faith*
[86] *Reformed*
[87] *Büdingen, Hesse*
[88] ibid
[89] Merian, Matthew, *Büdingen*
[90] Pleve, Igor. R., *The German Colonies on the Volga*, p. 139
[91] ibid, p. 141
[92] Mai, Brent Alan, *1798 Census of the German Colonies along the Volga Vol 1*, pp. 37-40
[93] *80th Anniversary Of The Free Evangelical Lutheran Cross Church 1892-1972*, p. 6
[94] Geisinger, Adam, *From Catherine to Krushchev: The Story of Russia's Germans*, p. 156-157
[95] ibid, p. 201
[96] *Religion*
[97] Cellar, Konrad, *The German colonies in South Russia*, pp. 110-111

[98] Pleve, Igor. R., *The German Colonies on the Volga*, p. 283
[99] Pisarevskii, G.G., "*Internal Order in the Volga Colonies under Catherine II,*" p. XVI
[100] Gutsche, Horst W., *Katherinenstadt Church in 1997*, p. 39
[101] *80th Anniversary Of The Free Evangelical Lutheran Cross Church 1892-1972*
[102] *ibid*, p. 14
[103] *ibid*, p. 13
[104] *ibid*, p. 148
[105] Gutsche, Horst W., *Katherinenstadt Church in 1997*, p. 38
[106] *ibid*, p. 21
[107] *80th Anniversary Of The Free Evangelical Lutheran Cross Church 1892-1972*, p. 17
[108] Scherbakovka Church
[109] Gutsche, Horst W., *Katherinenstadt Church in 1997*, p. 23
[110] *80th Anniversary Of The Free Evangelical Lutheran Cross Church 1892-1972*, p. 15
[111] *ibid*, p. 9
[112] White, Sharon, *Warenburg Church 2003*
[113] *80th Anniversary Of The Free Evangelical Lutheran Cross Church 1892-1972*, p. 9
[114] White, Sharon, *Warenburg Church 2003*
[115] Hoffman, Stefanie, *From Puppets of Stalin to Pawns of Hitler & Back Again*, p.10
[116] Williams, Hattie Plum, The Czar's Germans, p. 175
[117] Harms, Wilmer A., *Insights Into Russia*, p.16
[118] Haynes, Emma S., *A History of the Volga Relief Society*, p.28
[119] Geisinger, Adam, *From Catherine to Krushchev: The Story of Russia's Germans*, p. 243
[120] *80th Anniversary Of The Free Evangelical Lutheran Cross Church 1892-1972*, p. 142
[121] Gaer, Joseph, *What the Great Religions Believe*, p.16
[122] White, Sharon, *German Tombstone in Warenburg Cemetery in 2003*

Made in the USA
San Bernardino, CA
22 February 2020